BREAK FREE FROM STRESS

From Chaos to Calm

AF603821

POONAM MADAAN

Copyright © Poonam Madaan 2022
All Rights Reserved.

ISBN 979-8-88883-655-2

This book has been published with all efforts taken to make the material error-free after the consent of the author. However, the author and the publisher do not assume and hereby disclaim any liability to any party for any loss, damage, or disruption caused by errors or omissions, whether such errors or omissions result from negligence, accident, or any other cause.

While every effort has been made to avoid any mistake or omission, this publication is being sold on the condition and understanding that neither the author nor the publishers or printers would be liable in any manner to any person by reason of any mistake or omission in this publication or for any action taken or omitted to be taken or advice rendered or accepted on the basis of this work. For any defect in printing or binding the publishers will be liable only to replace the defective copy by another copy of this work then available.

Contents

Acknowledgement

I would like to thank God for the following:

- For this beautiful life, filled with a variety of learnings and experiences
- For blessing me with a lovely family. My Inspiration: My dear husband Manoj and lovely daughters Yashasvi and Mishika.
- For giving me the opportunity to spread smiles through my words, written and spoken.

Disclaimer

This book is not therapy or counselling and does not provide clinical advice and treatment. We advise readers dealing with medical or mental health issues to consult their physicians and professional service providers. Activities in this book are not medically proven to benefit everyone. The effect may vary from person to person. You can skip a particular activity if:

1. you have any past traumatic memories related to the activity, or

2. you have been medically advised to avoid it.

The publisher and author take no responsibility for any unwanted consequences from the application of activities and information in this book.

**‘It’s not the load that breaks you down,
it’s the way you carry it.’**

Lou Holtz

Preface

The desire to help people and bring smile on their face inspired me to write this book.

I have worked hard on this book to collate the simple stress-buster activities in the most straightforward language. This book is a result of 5 years of extensive research, which is still ongoing. After personally using these activities to break free from stress, I happily offer them to my readers. I consider this book a significant milestone in my mission to spread smiles.

I am not a medical professional. My expertise in writing this book originates from my good and bad life experiences. The good experiences have helped me to survive and enjoy life. Whereas the bad experiences were my teachers who taught me the best lessons to build strength & courage, they shaped my personality and made me what I am today.

This book is not to read but to follow.

At times of stress, this book will be your best buddy. It is a collection of simple activities to de-stress. When the stress levels are high, diverting attention for some time helps.

'When you can't change the situation,
change the situation.'

This book follows the same approach and helps to divert attention and engage the mind in something productive. It is not meant to be read in a single sitting; instead, it has to be used as a ready reference whenever under stress.

There are two ways to read this book:

1. Page for the day: Read a page every morning and follow it during the day when the need arises.
2. Best buddy: Whenever stressed, randomly open the book and follow the activity that shows up.

This book contains resources that can help you break free from stress. You will start noticing positive changes in you after regular use for one month.

(If you come across a page which is difficult to follow, just open another page.)

We all are blessed with the inner resources to become anything we want to be. Realizing this, some pages are kept blank in the book; the readers can use them to mention the resources they personally use to de-stress during difficult times.

At the end of each activity, there is space to write your experience while doing the activity.

Be as creative as you can while writing.

Hoping this book reaches those who need it at the right time.

Keep Smiling!

Break Free From Stress

Poonam Madaan

'Take time to do what makes your soul happy.'

Doodle Something on Paper

Time to doodle!

Wherever you are, you just have to find a paper and a pen/pencil. Start making anything on the Paper. Make what comes to your mind. It can be a star, a drop, a flower, a leaf or any random image of any size, big or small or a combination of both big and small.

Fill the whole page with your imagination and creativity. If it's difficult to imagine any shape or design, just scribble. Don't look for perfection; it is the last thing expected when doodling. Keep drawing without applying mind.

Empty your mind on the Paper. Doodle freestyle until you feel comfortable.

We all must have done doodling during our school times, mainly on the last page of all notebooks. Some people love to write words, some love to draw images, some love to try different signatures, and some draw different geometrical shapes. Just go back to that time and be that kid once. Draw with complete focus on the pen and Paper only.

Be in the flow and completely forget everything around you; just be with your pen and paper for a while.

While you are doodling, the only thing that should occupy your mind should be what to draw next. The only thought that persists should be the thought of doodling.

Keep repeating the designs and patterns to make it easy. Look around and see if you can copy any design. Remain focused for at least 5 minutes, don't stop if you are in a flow.

Once done, stop and have a look at your creativity with a gentle smile.

Close your eyes, and take some slow and deep breaths. Feel the changes in your body.

Open your eyes and get back to work refreshed!

Time taken for this activity: 5 to 10 minutes

'Fake it until you make it.'

Thumbs Up and Smile

Time to cheer up!

Show your thumbs up with your fist closed as if you wish yourself all the best; now add a smile to this posture. If you want to have a better experience, close your eyes. Hold this pose for at least 20 seconds (and more if you wish to). Feel the change in your body when you smile.

Smiling is the most positive body expression, and it generates feel-good hormones that help to elevate the mood instantly. I am sure you have also felt that change immediately. Just observe and experience the changes in your body. Entirely focus on what is happening inside. You may feel some sensation around a specific area in your body; it could be your chest, stomach, or face. Observe the movement and try to understand how it is moving inside your body.

- Is it going up or down?
- Is it moving in circles?
- In which direction is it moving; right to left or left to right?
- Which part of your body has maximum sensation?

- How is your breathing; fast, slow or regular?

Keep smiling with your eyes closed and feel the internal sensations. Smile is the instant mood lifter. A smile is good physiologically, psychologically and socially. A fake or real smile generates the same feelings in the body. And a positive body posture is just like a cherry on the cake. When the head is held high with a smile, you are ready to conquer any problem. Power poses are proven to affect feelings and, in turn, thoughts positively.

A power pose with a smile is a sure shot to break free from stress.

Time taken for this activity: 1 to 2 minutes

‘Happy times come and go, but the memories stay forever. Cherish those memories.’

Recall a Happy Memory

Time to visit the happy memory!

For a moment, just forget everything around you, close your eyes and go back to your past to find a specific event when you were thrilled. So happy, as if on cloud 9. Take some time to recall such a moment in your life. It could be any event from your past, big or small; it doesn't matter.

That moment when you were the happiest, whose memory you cherish, and it brings a big smile to your face even today, that moment you want to experience again and again. It could be when:

- you cleared an exam for which you prepared very hard, or
- you got your dream job in your dream company, or
- you got married to the love of your life, or
- you became a parent and held your baby in your hands for the first time, or
- you went for a vacation or
- any other such moment that you cherish.

If you cannot find such an event, try to create a moment in your mind. Imagine a situation when you would be the happiest.

Once you are able to find that moment, close your eyes and make the experience alive in your mind by recalling each detail. Visit that point in your life and be a part of that moment. See what you saw at that time, feel what you felt and hear what you heard. Completely immerse in that moment and experience it thoroughly. Feel good; intensify the joy by thinking about all the happy things that happened to you at that moment, and see the tears of joy in everyone's eyes. Recall how those around you felt. Experience the positive changes in your body.

Feel happy and satisfied. Thank God for all that happened, and be grateful to all those who made that happy moment possible. Open your eyes when you are comfortable.

Time taken for this activity: 5 to 10 minutes

'Deep breaths are like little love notes to your body.'

Take Deep Breaths

Time to breathe deep!

Close your eyes, and put one hand on your chest and one on your belly. Once you establish a connection with your inner self, inhale slowly, smoothly and deeply. Feel the air flowing down your nostrils entering your windpipe, chest, and lungs. Once you feel the air filled in your lungs, exhale slowly. Focus on the air moving in and out through your nose.

With each breath, observe the movement in your body. The belly should move with each breath, and the chest should be almost static. With each inhalation, fill in the air and inflate the abdomen; deflate and move it in with each exhalation.

Keep in mind to engage your stomach more during the process and avoid moving the upper part of your body.

- Don't breathe with force.
- Don't make any sound from the nose during the process.
- Don't breathe from the chest.

Do at least ten rounds of deep breathing, where one round starts from inhalation through the nose and ends at exhalation through the same.

RELAX your body more and more with each breath. With each inhalation, feel the joy and happiness entering your body. Feel the energy transferred to each cell of your body.

With each exhalation, feel the tensions and worries moving out. Feel lighter and observe the positive change in your body. The increased oxygen supply and mental and physical relaxation will refresh you.

Time taken for this activity: 3 to 5 minutes

‘Stop, stare and give yourself the much needed break.’

Stare an Object

Time to stare!

Stop, leave all the work in hand and relax on your chair. Now, find a point around you where you can continuously stare without any distraction and discomfort. It can be any area around you where the light is not too bright. The point can be a plain wall, a wall hanging, a painting on the wall, or any furniture. If you are in some open area, it can be a flower, a tree, a pillar or anything you can find comfortable to stare at. Once you are satisfied with the point of focus (that may be finalised after some attempts), pay attention and focus entirely on that point.

Remember not to select any moving thing to stare at, like a pet, car, fan, clock, etc. This activity will give good results when you stare at something that does not distract your attention through movement.

Keep staring for at least two minutes or more if you feel comfortable. While you are staring, start observing the area around that point without moving your eyes away. Keep your eyes focused on the point and notice the things around them. This exercise will not only help you to break from stress but will also enhance your peripheral vision.

You can blink your eyes when you feel like it but hold the stare. When you feel heaviness in the eyes or start feeling sleepy, you can shift the point and continue this activity with the new point.

This activity can also be called open-eye meditation and can be quickly done anywhere at any time. Similar activity is used in hypnotism to control the other person's mind. Some people also use this activity to fall asleep.

You may feel sleepy after this activity; it's OK to close your eyes and nap while sitting on the chair. Open your eyes when comfortable, and feel refreshed and ready to conquer your problems.

Time taken for this activity: 3 to 5 minutes

‘Tension is who you think you should be. Relaxation is who you are.’

Progressive Muscle Relaxation

Time to relax and rejuvenate!

Sit comfortably in your chair (if possible, lie down), relax and close your eyes. Focus on your breathing; breathe slowly and deeply. Inhale and inflate your stomach; exhale and deflate it. Do not force the breath; let it be a slow and gradual process. Relax and count backwards from 10 to 1; with each number, relax more and more.

Once you are entirely relaxed, breathe in and start tightening your body. Tense the muscles of each body part, starting from the feet and slowly moving up. Squeeze the muscles of your calf, thighs, pelvic area, stomach, arms, hands, chest, shoulders, neck and face. Keep tightening it more are more with each inhalation. Keep inhaling and exhaling slowly and deeply throughout the process. Hold the tension for 10 seconds. Focus entirely on what is happening inside your body.

After holding the tension for at least 10 seconds, start releasing each muscle slowly. Loosen them and, with each exhalation, release the tension more and more. Notice the difference between tensed and relaxed muscles. Observe the changes in the body, the feeling of warmth and the difference in the blood flow.

Relax for 10 seconds, and count backwards from 10 to 1. Repeat the entire process three times. Identify any specific muscle group that needs more relaxation; repeat the process only for that particular body part.

Remember not to squeeze the muscles too hard; you should not feel pain or cramps while tensing the muscles. Do the entire exercise slowly and smoothly.

This exercise may take 5 minutes when done at once for the whole body, but if you have time, do this exercise by focusing on one muscle group or body part at a time. Like start with feet only, inhale and squeeze the muscles of the feet, hold for 10 seconds and then release, wait for 10 seconds and move on to the calf muscles; repeat the same process and keep moving up. It may take 15 to 20 minutes and will be more effective.

Time taken for this activity: 10 to 20 minutes

‘When your body surrenders to movement, your soul remembers its dance.’

Gabrielle Roth

Move your Shoulders

Time to move!

Relax and close your eyes. Focus on your breath; breathe in and out slowly and sync your breathing with the movement in the body. Once you are comfortable, bring your focus to your shoulders. Move them up slowly, raise them towards your ears and try to touch your ear lobes with your shoulders; stay at this position for 5 seconds and then move down slowly. Keep doing it slowly five more times. Once done for five times, stop and relax for 10 seconds. Feel the change in your body, and observe the warmth and other sensations in your upper body, especially in the chest area.

Imagine dancing to some music and swaying your body with the shoulder movement. Repeat these steps with increased speed. Gradually keep on increasing the speed and keep repeating the action. You can also add different shoulder movements.

If you want, you can switch on the music of your choice along with the activity and try to match the shoulder movement to the music. Do this activity for at least 2 minutes or until you feel comfortable.

You will notice positive changes in your body; your body may feel lighter and refreshed.

Remember not to injure yourself during the activity; keep an eye on your body and stop whenever you feel discomfort.

Time taken for this activity: 2 to 5 minutes

‘Touch the body, heal the mind, calm the spirit.’

Press All Fingers One by One

Time for reflexology!

Leave all the work and be empty-handed. Wrap the little finger of your left hand around the index finger of your other hand, so it's fully enveloped and nestled in your palm. You may feel a light pulsation. It isn't necessary to close your eyes, but you can if that feels best. The point is to feel comfortable. Press the finger and keep moving the pressure over the finger, from up to down and vice versa. Keep pressing the finger slowly for 10 seconds.

Now, move on to the left hand's ring finger and repeat the same process. Spend 10 seconds on each finger and focus on the pressure exerted on the finger from top to bottom. Keep moving to the next finger and follow the same process with each finger of both hands.

Once all fingers have been massaged, it's time to press the fingernails. Start from the fingernail of the little finger of the left hand. Hold the fingernail tightly between the index finger and thumb of the other hand. Keep pressing firmly and hold the pressure for 5 seconds. Focus on the sensations in the fingernail due to the pressure. Keep moving to the next finger and follow the same process for all fingernails.

Now, hold the little finger of the left hand in between the thumb and index finger of the other hand and rotate the little finger gently between the grip. Keep turning for 5 seconds and move on to the next finger. Follow the same steps for all the fingers of both hands.

It is a very effective Japanese technique to break free from stress.

Time taken for this activity: 3 to 5 minutes

'We don't laugh because we are happy, we are happy because we laugh.'

William James

Laugh Silently

Time to laugh!

Stop all work in hand. Relax, take a deep breath, close your eyes, gently smile and hold this smile for 5 seconds. Bring your attention to your present moment.

Now start giggling with your mouth shut and without making any sound. Move your abdomen while laughing. Gradually increase the intensity of the giggles and turn them into laughter.

Laugh as if you are trying to hide your laugh from others. There should be no sound, but the whole body has to be engaged in the laughter. Move your shoulders up and down, move your stomach in and out and make the smile wider.

Keep laughing for 20 seconds or till you are comfortable. Pause for 10 seconds. During the pause, focus on the changes in the body. Identify the areas having maximum sensation. Focus on the feeling of positivity. Keep the smile intact during the entire activity.

Start the same steps after the pause—silent laughter for 20 seconds and pause for 10 seconds. Do at least five rounds of silent laughter.

Relax your entire body and feel the positive changes taking place inside the body.

Laughter increases the oxygen supply to the body and makes it feel refreshed. It also produces feel-good hormones that elevate positivity, relieve pain and helps to break free from stress.

Time taken for this activity: 2 to 5 minutes

‘Thousands have lived without love, not one without water.’

W.H.Auden

Drink a Glass of Water

Time to water yourself!

Stop all work and relax. Think about a glass of fresh water, and visualise how it looks. Get up and get your glass of fresh drinking water. Avoid drinking from a bottle and take a glass. Find someplace to sit and be comfortable.

Get your glass of water in your hands; wait, don't drink it. Look at the water and observe what is going on inside the glass. Do you see any water bubble? See how the water is moving inside the glass. Observe it for 5 to 10 seconds. Think only about water at this time. Close your eyes and visualise the water glass that you are holding in your hands.

Open your eyes and take a small sip of refreshing water. Feel the touch of water on your lips. Don't gulp it at once; take it in slowly and feel the water moving inside your body. Close your eyes and feel the water going down from your lips to the tongue, throat and food pipe till it gets dissolved inside. With closed eyes, focus entirely on the water moving inside your body. Observe it till the last point and feel refreshed.

Now, open your eyes and take the next sip. Follow the same process with each sip. Maintain the slow pace and feel each sip from entry in your body till it entirely gets dissolved inside. Feel the refreshing feeling with each sip. Spend some quality time with your glass of water. Think only about the water and focus on how it interacts with your body. When you start feeling full, stop drinking more water.

Say thanks to water for filling you up and satisfying your thirst.

Feel refreshed!

Time taken for this activity: 2 - 5 minutes

‘Sometimes, music is the only medicine that the heart & soul needs.’

Hum Any Tune

Time for some music!

Find a place where you can be yourself and others won't get disturbed by your voice. Once settled, think about your favourite song or any song you repeatedly hear. Close your eyes, take a deep breath and relax. Start playing the music in your mind, listen to the song pay attention to the song's lyrics and video (if any). Keep playing the song in your mind with your eyes closed. Immerse yourself in the song completely. Slowly, start following the music and start humming along. Once in the flow, start to sing the song too. Keep humming and enjoy the song.

Let your body also accompany you. Move your head, tap your feet, clap your hands or snap your fingers. Sway your body with the music. Keep a gentle smile on your face throughout this activity.

Don't worry about your external environment at this time. Be fully immersed in the rhythm and follow it.

Keep humming and feel the positive shift in your body from head to toe. With your eyes closed, start observing each part of your body and feel how you have engaged each body part in this activity. When you feel comfortable, open your eyes and thank your body for this wondrous feeling.

Feel energetic and ready to rock!

Time taken for this activity: 2 - 5 minutes

"I have got ice water running through my veins, I'm cool."

Dean Ambrose

Hands in a Bowl of Ice

Time to freeze!

Get up and find your way to the kitchen or pantry. Search for a big bowl that can easily accommodate both your hands inside. Now, open the refrigerator and search for the ice. Take at least ten ice cubes from the tray and put them in the bowl. Pour little water into it, don't fill the bowl and leave enough space to fit in your hands without spilling water.

Come back to a sitting position, close your eyes, take a deep breath and relax. Open your eyes and slowly start dipping your hands in the bowl. You can either start with one hand at a time or both hands together. Take 5 to 10 seconds to dip both hands till your wrist. Feel the chill of the water in your hands and observe the body sensations in response to the temperature change.

Once the hands are fully immersed till the wrist, hold them in, count to five and slowly take out your hands. Keep them out for 5 seconds and again dip your hands; increase the count this time and dip your hands for 10 seconds. Take out and count till 5. Again dip your hands for 10 seconds, and take them out. Repeat this process at least five times, dip for 10 seconds and keep out for 5 seconds.

Remember to keep a gentle smile on your face during the entire activity. Focus on the sensations in and around your hands. The changes in your body that accompany the changes in your hands. Once done, wipe your hands, sit back and close your eyes. Don't move, and bring your body to your usual position. When you are ready, open your eyes and get ready to conquer the world with a smile.

Time taken for this activity: 5 - 10 minutes

‘Life is a song, sing it.’

Mother Teresa

Listen to Your Favourite Song

Time for a song!

Find a place where you are comfortable. Take out your earphones, connect them to your device and put them on. (If you are in a place where you can switch on the song without earphones, you can do it, but earphones will provide a better experience.)

Select a song with beautiful memories linked to it—the piece whose music and lyrics help to boost your mood. Once selected, play the song on your device. Don't take too much time to choose the song, do it fast.

Close your eyes and pay attention to hearing the song. Focus on each word of the song. Be in the present moment and immerse yourself entirely in the music. Try to recall the visuals (video) of the song if you can. Pay attention to the rhythm and be in the flow. Enjoy the song to the core.

Experience the emotions and memories (if any) related to the song, and let your body react. Feel the changes in your body and acknowledge them.

Relax and hear the song once more; try to sing along and dance if you can. Go back to when you listened to this song for the first time, and you loved to hear it again and again.

Play the song in a loop and hear it till you feel satisfied. Keep a gentle smile on your face during the whole activity. Let the eyes be closed full-time. When you are comfortable, open your eyes and thank the song for making your moments beautiful.

Time taken for this activity: 5 - 10 minutes

‘When you dance to your own rhythm, life taps its toes to your beat.’

Terri Guillemets

Tap Your Feet in a Rhythm

Time to tap your feet!

Just stop all work for a moment, sit back and relax. Take a deep and slow breath, and look up with your head facing the ceiling or the sky. Try to recall some rhythm or create one. Play the rhythm in your mind. It can be any song's rhythm, even a nursery rhyme, or a simple 1, 2, cha, cha, cha, 3, 4, cha, cha, cha.

Once you are ready with the rhythm, start playing it in your mind. Start tapping your feet with the rhythm. Tap one by one or both feet together. Follow the rhythm that is playing in your mind. Keep tapping for 10 seconds and, take a pause, repeat it ten times.

Keep the movement very gentle and comfortable. The feet should be flat on the ground to make them more comfortable. Keep the heel touched to the floor and move only the front part of the feet. Let the leg and feet be free.

If you feel comfortable, slowly lift your entire feet also in between and tap them gently on the ground. Keep adding some hand and body movements with the process to immerse fully into the experience. Sway your body, move your shoulders, turn your head or swing your arms. Add on any dance move too.

Keep your eyes closed during the process, if possible, and have a gentle smile on your face throughout.

After repeating at least ten times, stop moving, relax on your seat with your eyes closed, gentle smile, and slow breathing. Bring your attention to the sensation in your feet. Feel the warmth in your sole and legs.

Open your eyes when comfortable, and thank your body and mind.

Time taken for this activity: 3 - 5 minutes

‘Make peace with your broken pieces.’

R.H.Sin

Tear Paper into Pieces

Time to tear it off!

Find some paper and scissors; it is OK if you can't find scissors. You can also take a newspaper if it is readily available. Sit back on your chair, relax, close your eyes and take a deep breath. Gently open your eyes, take the Paper in your hand and observe it. Pick up the scissor and cut the Paper from one side into small pieces. If you don't have scissors, tear them with your hands.

Keep cutting or tearing the paper into small pieces. Make as many small pieces as you can. Keep collecting the small bits at a place, so it's easy to wind up after the activity. Enjoy the process, and keep a gentle smile during the exercise.

Take more Paper once you are done and cut it into small pieces. You can also try cutting it in different shapes. It can be any shape that comes to your mind.

Let your mind be free of any thoughts during the process. Just focus entirely on tearing or cutting paper into pieces. Hear the sound made by the scissors while cutting Paper or the sound made while tearing it off. Enjoy the sound and notice the difference when you increase your speed. Keep changing your speed while tearing or cutting Paper.

Once you have completed the cutting, relax and see the small pieces. Observe the different shapes formed and be with the pieces for a moment; close your eyes, breathe deep and relax.

Take the pieces and throw them in the trash.

Feel lighter and refreshed!

Time taken for this activity: 3 - 5 minutes

‘Appreciation is a wonderful thing, it makes what is excellent in others belong to us as well.’

Appreciate Someone

Time to appreciate!

Look around you and find someone with whom you are comfortable talking. If you can't find someone around you, search the contact list on your phone, identify a person you can call, and carry on this activity.

Once you identify the person, call them or go to them and start casual talk with them. Be comfortable and focus only on speaking something positive. Do not discuss any negative topic.

When you feel comfortable during the talk, divert the topic slowly towards appreciating the other person. While appreciating, focus entirely on sharing what good things you have noticed in them and how you feel about them.

Remember, the appreciation should look genuine. It should not appear as flattery or flirting, and the other person should feel happy about being appreciated.

The appreciation has to come from your heart, and your body language should be in sync with your words of appreciation. To know if you are genuinely appreciating, check how you feel while complementing another person. If you feel good during the process, then it's a genuine effort. When we appreciate from the heart, the connection strengthens, and we feel good. Sincere appreciation makes both persons happy, the receiver and the speaker.

Keep a gentle smile on your face during the activity. You can also use hand gestures, like patting the back of the other person or pressing their hands to make them feel good. Avoid touching them if you are unsure how the other person may feel. Do not judge them on how they react. Do not try to infringe on their personal space by asking any personal questions or giving any advice.

Once you are comfortable, make a proper closure, take their permission and leave with gratitude. Feel happy and charged!

Time taken for this activity: 5 - 10 minutes

'Nobody can make you happy, unless you are happy with yourself first.'

Appreciate Yourself

Time for self-praise!

Leave all work, relax, close your eyes and take a deep breath. Think of one thing that you like about yourself. It can be a skill, talent, strength or something that makes you exceptional. Think of a quality that people appreciate the most in you.

Now, find a mirror around you where you can stand comfortably with complete privacy; if you can't find a mirror, then use your phone selfie camera. Face towards the mirror, look into your eyes and smile gently. Fill your heart with a genuine appreciation for yourself. Control your mind only to think good at this time. Think of the one line that you can speak to appreciate and love yourself. Keep your hand on your heart, look into your eyes and say it.

For example, you can say, 'Poonam (your name), you are awesome/so talented/so caring/so brilliant/a wonderful mother (whatever you want to appreciate yourself for)".

Gently close your eyes, be fully in the moment and experience the changes in your body. Let the emotions flow freely; they may also flow like tears.

When you are comfortable, open your eyes and smile.

Again look into the mirror, see into your eyes, keep one hand on your heart, and smile gently. This time say these lines, "**I am** awesome/so talented/so caring/a wonderful mother". Gently close your eyes, be fully in the present moment and experience the changes in your body.

Open your eyes when you are comfortable and smile. Look in the mirror, smile and say, 'I love you.' Do this activity as many times as you can during the day.

Time taken for this activity: 5 - 10 minutes

‘ABILITY is what you are capable of doing, MOTIVATION determines what you do and ATTITUDE determines how well you do it.’

Read a Motivational Quote

Time to get motivated!

Relax, close your eyes and take a deep breath. Think of a famous person who always motivates you. Now, open google and search for a motivational quote from them. If you cannot find such a person, then randomly search for a motivational quote.

Select a quote that appeals to you, and you feel empowered after reading it. Read that quote once more and close your eyes. Repeat that quote to yourself and focus on the meaning of the quote. Try to assess how it relates to your life. Think of a reason why you liked that quote. Go deeper and dig out a situation where this quote helped you move ahead. Pay attention to your body, and assess how you feel right now. Just be in the present moment and experience the quote's power.

Open your eyes and write this quote somewhere. Place it somewhere where you can see it easily. It can be a board on your work desk or your mobile home screen, or your computer desktop background.

You can also identify a motivational quote that has always inspired you, frame it and keep it where you can often see it during the day. This quote can be a source of external motivation and may help you to get inspiration for the day.

Feel the power of the quote and get motivated to move ahead.

Time taken for this activity: 3 to 5 minutes

‘It’s OK to say No, without explaining yourself.’

Move Your Head in a 'No'

Time to say 'No'!

Leave all the work in hand for a moment, sit back on a chair, close your eyes, take a deep breath and relax. Bring your attention to your breath and the movement in your body. When you inhale, the stomach should go out, and when you exhale, the stomach should go in. Try to correct the body movement as per the breathing pattern and let the breathing and body movement be in sync.

When completely relaxed, close your eyes and slowly move your head from right to left and left to right. Pretend as if you are saying 'No' to someone. Stop for some time and think of a situation where you strongly want to say 'No' but cannot. If you cannot find it, imagine a situation where you would like to say no. It could be in your professional life or personal life.

Keep your eyes closed during the activity. Once you find such a situation, visualise yourself in that situation. Experience it, see what you saw, hear what you heard and feel what you felt. Feel the urge to say no in the case; identify your emotion. Is it anger, resentment, jealousy or frustration? Feel the emotion in your body; once you can visualise the right time to say no, move your head in a 'No'. If possible, shout saying, 'No'. Say it at least three times. Stop and feel the change in your body.

Come back to your present; when you are comfortable, open your eyes and feel the change.

Time taken for this activity: 3 to 5 minutes

‘We don’t stop playing because we grow old, we grow old because we stop playing.’

George Bernard Shaw

Play a Game

Time to play!

Can you think of a game that you can play now? It can be any game, preferably not virtual. Many games can be played with paper and a pen, like tic tac toe, dots and boxes, hangman, dumb charades, etc. You can also play games like card games, board games, etc. As most of these games need one more player, ask someone who can be a game partner with you.

If nothing comes to mind or you cannot find someone who can be a game partner, search for a virtual game you can play alone, like candy crush, word builder, etc.

Once you have selected the game and are ready to play, be fully engaged. While playing, focus only on the game, don't be distracted. Just think about how you can play the game well and try to be a winner. Enjoy every moment of the game. If other people want to join, pool them in and enjoy with them. Avoid any discussions other than the game in hand. Purely be a game player. Focus on winning the game and enjoying and playing it to the fullest.

When you win, experience the joy of winning; when you lose, experience the joy of the other person.

Congratulate yourself when you win, and congratulate the other person on their win—play for as long as you are comfortable playing.

Once you have played the game and are satisfied, sit back on your chair, close your eyes, take a deep breath, have a gentle smile and observe the sensations in your body. Feel lighter and happier with every breath. Remember that life is a game; enjoy it fully.

Time taken for this activity: 10 to 15 minutes

‘As I say yes to life, life says yes to me.’

Louise Hay

Move Your Head in a 'Yes'

Time to say Yes!

Leave all work in hand, take a break and find a place where you can relax without distractions. Sit down and relax, close your eyes, keep both hands on your thighs with palms facing up, take a slow deep breath, inhale and exhale slowly and smoothly. Keep a gentle smile on your face throughout the activity.

Think of a moment in your life when you desperately wanted to say Yes, but could not. With your eyes closed, slowly move your head from up to down. Do it five times and then stop. Take some time to reflect, go down your memory lane and try to pick out the situation. If you cannot find such a situation, imagine a situation where you want to say yes but find it difficult to say. It can be any situation in your imagination; go as wild as possible.

Once you can find such a situation, visualise it in your mind, see what you saw in the situation, hear what you heard and feel what you felt. Play the entire scene in your mind. Come to the point where you have a strong urge to say yes. Gather all your courage and move your head in affirmation. If you are in a comfortable environment, say loudly 'Yes'. If you want, you can say it more than once.

Once you are satisfied, come back to your present and observe the changes in your body. When you are comfortable, open your eyes, smile and feel the power to say yes.

Time taken for this activity: 3 to 5 minutes

‘Every time we eat, it’s an opportunity to nourish our body.’

Eat Something You Love

Time to eat what you love!

Leave all work in hand, get up and get ready to grab something your stomach desires. If you are at a place where you have easy access to food items, then go to the area and find something you love to eat. If not, then use an app to order online.

Once you are ready with the food, pause and observe the food. Smell it, see it and imagine the taste of the food. Let your mouth salivate, and let your body crave it. Control yourself for at least 30 seconds and only experience the company of your favourite food.

Take a small bite and don't chew it, just keep it in your mouth. Close your eyes and feel the food's texture, taste and smell. Now, start chewing it slowly; chew it thoroughly before swallowing. Remember to keep your eyes closed during the process. When you eat the food, focus on the movement of food inside your body. Feel it going down your throat to the food pipe. Feel the satisfaction when it reaches your stomach.

Feel grateful for the food. Now continue eating the rest of the food following the same process. Be slow and mindful. When eating, focus entirely on the food, spend time only on eating, engage all senses to experience the food and enjoy each bite to the core.

Time taken for this activity: 10 to 15 minutes approx.

‘Good food is all the tastier, when shared with good friends.’

Treat Someone to a Dessert

Time to give a treat!

Get ready, leave all your work, relax and think of a dessert that most of the people around you love to have and can be easily sourced by you now. If you live where online delivery is available, prefer to order online. Else, go to the store and buy something delicious.

Once you have the food with you, look for someone who will be happy to accompany you and with whom you can happily share the dessert. Reach out to them and invite them to join you. Politely ask them if they would like to accompany you as you would love to treat them and spend some time with them.

Find a comfortable place and offer them dessert. Be fully present and engage yourself in the conversation with the person. Take care when they need more and pay attention to their needs while eating. Accompany them in eating and appreciate the food and their company.

Now, if you cannot find someone with whom you can eat, don't worry. Take the dessert and offer it to someone who may love to have it but cannot afford it. It can be a security guard, driver, housekeeping person, office assistant, supporting staff at home or office, or even a beggar down the street.

Offer the dessert to them and see them savouring it. If you like, buy more to serve some more people. Feel the happiness of feeding someone. Make someone happy by feeding them something special.

The best memories of our life are related to either good people, good times or good food.

Once you are satisfied, come back to your place, relax, close your eyes and think about the happiness in the eyes of the other person whom you treated. Feel good and visualise the sparkle in the other person's eyes. Smile gently and thank the almighty for empowering you to share food and spread happiness.

Once you are comfortable, open your eyes and get back to work.

Time taken for this activity: Min. 15 to 20 minutes (approx.)

‘Sometimes having fun is all the best therapy you need.’

Make a Funny Face

Time to have fun!

Leave all your work and get ready to look silly. Close your eyes, take a deep breath and relax. If you are uncomfortable doing this activity in your seat, move to a comfortable place. Find an area with a mirror, or use your phone selfie camera. You can also use the washroom for this activity.

Once you are ready, think of a funny or silly facial expression and try to imitate it. Try as many postures as you can. If you are not able to recall any silly facial expressions, then read the below list to help you find many:

- Do some uncoordinated movements of the facial features
- Move your eyebrows up and down many times
- Smile, hold for 3 seconds, stop and be serious, repeat it
- Open your mouth and pull it from both ends with your fingers
- Make a pout; move your pout in different directions

- Stick out your tongue with your eyebrows moving up
- Open your mouth widely and hold
- Make a surprised face
- Make a grumpy face
- See yourself in the mirror and give an expression of shyness
- Make a scared face
- Assume yourself to be a kid and act as they do
- Assume yourself to be an animal, make different sounds and act like them

If nothing works, search for some silly faces on google and try to imitate them.

Once you are satisfied, close your eyes and smile. Laugh if you feel like it. With your eyes closed, observe the changes in your body.

Feel the positive vibes; when you are comfortable, open your eyes and return to work.

Time taken for this activity: 3 to 5 minutes (approx.)

‘Mantra is a word of power and light. It energizes the body, purifies the mind, cleans the soul and evokes true positive change.’

Chant a Mantra

It's time for chanting!

Get ready with a mantra that is small and easy to recite. It can be as small as one word. If you cannot remember any mantra, think of some positive words like relax, calm, etc. You can also think of positive affirmations like I am joyful, I am peaceful, etc.

Once you are ready with a mantra, relax and sit comfortably in a quiet place with no distractions. Decide how long you want to meditate and set the alarm at a low volume with a soothing sound. Close your eyes, have a gentle smile, relax and start with a few slow deep breaths.

Pay attention to the movement in your body with every breath. Focus on the sensation created through your breath passing from your nose to each internal body part until it reaches the lungs and comes out. Once you are in the meditative state, start reciting the mantra, say it slowly and focus on the sound & vibrations of the mantra. You can say it loudly or silently as per your comfort. Hear the sound of the mantra and focus on your lip movement when you recite it. Try to sync the mantra with your breathing, and let it flow in a rhythm. The rhythm will make you feel at ease.

As you meditate, your attention may wander, don't stop your thoughts; welcome them, park them for the time being and bring your attention back to the mantra. Continue till the alarm rings, and slowly get yourself back to this world. Open your eyes and sit with your quiet mind for some time. Observe the positive changes in your body.

When you are comfortable, come back to work with all the positivity.

Time taken for this activity: 5 to 30 minutes (approx.)

‘Humour is mankind’s greatest blessings.’

Mark Twain

Read a Joke

Time to be humorous!

Leave your work and get ready to tickle your funny bones. On your computer or mobile, open google and search for jokes. If you have a book on jokes, that will be the best thing as the chances of distraction will be reduced. Read the jokes and smile gently throughout the activity. Some jokes may make you laugh; don't stop yourself from laughing. If you dislike a joke, skip through it and move on to the next one. Work on developing your sense of humour by reading those jokes that make your humorous senses stronger. Don't try to find out any meaning from the jokes. Just read, smile and laugh if you are comfortable.

Keep saving the best jokes and make a collection for future reference. Next time when you have to redo this activity, you can simply scroll through the collection of these jokes and smile.

During this process, if someone around you gets intrigued, don't stop yourself from reading the joke to them. Share the joke with someone around or share it on social media at your convenience and spread smiles.

When you are comfortable, come back to work with all the positivity.

Time taken for this activity: 1 to 5 minutes (approx.)

‘If you could choose one characteristic that would get you through life, choose a sense of humour.’

Tell Someone a Joke

Time to spread smiles!

Leave your work and get ready to tickle your funny bones and those around you. Think of a joke you have recently come across and are comfortable sharing with someone in your style. If you can't recall any such joke, search online or from a book. Recall the joke or memorise it. Practice it once as to how you will share it with someone.

Once you are ready with the joke, start searching for the person you can share it comfortably. If you can't find someone around, think of someone you can call and share the joke with. Once you have identified the person, imagine how they will react to your joke. Keep a gentle smile on your face and visualise them smiling or laughing.

Now, get up from your seat and make an effort to connect with them. Initiate the talk and tell them you want to share a hilarious joke. Share the joke in your unique style by adding some humour to it. By any chance, if the other person doesn't find your joke too funny, then laugh to the point that you can't make them laugh. Feel free to laugh at yourself.

Laugh together and encourage them to share any joke or funny incident from their life. Spread positivity around.

When you are comfortable, come back to work with all the positive vibes.

Time taken for this activity: 2 to 5 minutes (approx.)

‘Honestly, shopping beats therapy, anytime. It costs the same and you get a dress out of it.’

Sophie Kinsella

Do Some Window Shopping

Time for shopping!

Yeah! Let's go shopping. But wait! Let's go for online window shopping. Open any shopping app on your phone or computer like Amazon, Flipkart, eBay, Myntra, etc. Think of something you want to buy and type in the search box. Start shortlisting the items and keep adding them to your wish list.

If nothing comes to your mind, then start searching for a dress. Type the dress of your choice in the search box and filter with the colour you like. Shortlist the one you would love to try on you. Once selected, just close your eyes and visualise yourself wearing that dress. Now, think about what accessories will enhance the look. Search for some accessories to match the dress, like jewellery, shoes, a bag, a watch, makeup, etc. Keep searching to complete your look.

Keep adding the items to your wish list, and then select the ones you want to team up with your chosen dress. Visualise yourself carrying the complete look. Feel good. Remember, it's only window shopping, so don't worry about the prices.

Once done, shut the screen, close your eyes and relax.

Time taken for this activity: 5 to 10 minutes (approx.)

‘The great advantage of a hotel room is that it is a refuge from routine life.’

George Bernard Shaw

Search for a Hotel Room

Yeah, time to travel.

Leave all the work in your hand, sit back and think of your dream destination for a vacation—a place where you would like to go on a long vacation with your favourite people. Now open a mobile travel app or a website on your laptop like MakeMyTrip, TripAdvisor, yatra, etc. Type in the name of the place in the search box, enter any date range and click on the find hotel button.

Search for some luxury options for a stay and shortlist the ones you like. Just open the hotel website and scroll through the gallery section for the selected ones. See the beautiful gardens, lavish hotel rooms and the luxury services offered by the hotel like spa, etc.

Now, close your eyes and recall the gallery images on the hotel website. Fit yourself in the pictures. See yourself in your best & comfortable outfit, roaming in the hotel park, swimming in the pool, having food in the best dining area, and sleeping on the neat and clean hotel bed. Sitting on the hotel balcony, enjoying your tea, reading your favourite book, enjoying spa services, etc.

Just think of the best way you chill out in a hotel on an extended break without any distractions. Just chill! Immerse in the hotel experience.

Open your eyes, smile, and return to work when comfortable. Feel refreshed, recharged and rejuvenated.

Time taken for this activity: 5 to 10 minutes (approx.)

‘Walk as if you are kissing the earth with your feet.’

Thich Nhat Hanh

Walk with Closed Eyes

Time to walk!

Stop your work, sit back and relax. Close your eyes and take some deep breaths. Keeping your eyes closed, stand up and walk around. Take small baby steps with closed eyes.

Feel the things around you with your hands and feet. Hear all the sounds around. Keep walking for some time, and be careful not to fall or bang on anything.

Be entirely in your present and observe everything around you with closed eyes. Feel everything with closed eyes and guess where you are and in which direction or location around your seat.

Once you are comfortable, think of the things you will see in front of you when you open your eyes. Think of at least five items that you can recall in front of you. Once you have the list, open your eyes and check if you are correct.

Repeat if you feel like doing it again!

Come back to your seat with closed eyes, smile and open your eyes when you feel comfortable.

Time taken for this activity: 5 to 10 minutes (approx.)

‘You are allowed to scream & cry, but do not give up.

Sometimes screaming is good for the heart.’

Scream into a Pillow

Time to scream!

Find a place where you can be yourself. Grab a pillow or towel for this activity.

Invite your negative thoughts, and experience the emotions that accompany these negative thoughts. Observe the changes in the body with these negative thoughts. Take a deep breath.

Experience the emotions of sadness, anger, guilt and jealousy, and just feel it. Let the emotions intensify. When the feelings peak, put your mouth in the pillow/towel and scream. Adequately cover your face to absorb the noise. Shout out loud inside the pillow and cry if you want. Don't stop the tears from rolling down. Keep shouting & crying till you feel comfortable.

Once done, drink a glass of water, slow down your breathing, close your eyes, take some deep breaths and relax. When comfortable, open your eyes and feel the change in your body.

Screaming is a scientifically acceptable means of expressing ourselves, but the pillow makes it a socially acceptable one, too.

Time taken for this activity: 5 to 10 minutes (approx.)

‘Cry as much as you want to, but just make sure, when you stop, you never cry for the same reason again.’

Cry Alone

Time to cry!

It's time to be face-to-face with the sadness in your heart. Get ready to face these hidden emotions.

Find a comfortable place where you can be truly yourself. Take a glass of water with you. Place yourself comfortably on a seat. Close your eyes, take a deep breath and connect to yourself. Go deep into your thoughts and discover those pent-up emotions you always try to hide from others. The thoughts and feelings you always run away from. You have become an expert in showing others that you are unaffected by these thoughts.

Let the feelings that are buried deep inside now come out. Let them come up and sit in front of you, talk to these feelings and try to understand why they want to show up. What do they want to convey to you? Why do they want to meet you again and again?

Feel the connection with these thoughts. Acknowledge the feelings, try to accept them and do not ignore them completely. Cry with them; let the tears roll down. Don't stop yourself. Vent out as much as you can. It is OK to cry for yourself. There is no one around you to judge or advise; you can be your true self.

Once you have no more thoughts to make you cry, stop. Drink a glass of water, soothe yourself and prepare yourself to face the world.

Time taken for this activity: 5 to 10 minutes (approx.)

‘There must be quite a few things that a hot bath won’t cure, but I don’t know many of them.’

Sylvia Plath

Take a Relaxing Warm Bath

Time to soak in the warmth of the water and relax!

Switch on the geyser and prepare yourself to take a bath. Once you are ready, switch on the tap and check if the water is warm enough. Stand under the shower and turn it on slowly. Soak yourself in the warm water. Each body part has to be covered with water from head to toe.

If you do not have a shower, fill a bucket with warm water, take a mug full of water and pour it slowly over your head. Place yourself safely and close your eyes. Keep running the water over your head and let it flow slowly from top to toe. Feel the water flowing down over your body. Feel the warmth of the water on each body part. Try to keep your eyes closed.

Visualise water washing away all your worries and tensions while flowing down. Open your eyes, take little water in your hand and pour it over your face. Fill it in your hand again, pour it over your arms, shoulders, chest area, stomach area, and legs, and move towards the toes.

Use your hands to gently rub the water all over your body, from top to toe. Close your eyes and feel your fingers' movement over your body. If you want, you can use soap to cleanse. If you have a bathtub, soak in it for some time. Pay attention to the body's sensations, and feel calmness and peace.

When comfortable, gently open your eyes. Pat dry yourself with a towel and get ready to face the world with a fresher you.

Time taken for this activity: 15 to 30 minutes (approx.)

‘Smash your Comfort Zone with cold showers.’

Take a Cold Bath

Time for a cold bath!

Are you getting chills already? No worries. Get up and get on the job.

Get yourself ready for the bath. Grab a towel and head towards the bathroom. Once ready to bath, stand under the shower, or fill the bucket with cold tap water. (Unless you have any health condition for which a cold bath is not recommended, you can freely take a cold bath).

Close your eyes, have a gentle smile and take some deep breaths. Open your eyes, slowly switch on the shower, or pour water over your head with the mug. Don't move aside or try to get away. Keep pouring the water over your head.

Close your eyes and feel the water moving down on your body from head to toe, touching each part of your body. You may feel chills at the start, but that is when you have to stay calm and let your entire body soak in the cold. Pour water on each body part and get completely drenched in the coldness.

After a while, when the body settles, you will no more feel the chills, and this is the time to enjoy the feeling of water touching your body. Focus only on the water and feel it flowing over your body.

Stop for a moment and start again. Do this five times.

Be playful and enjoy the water splashes; play with water and keep your smile intact. If you want, you can use soap and shampoo to cleanse.

Once done, switch off the water, wipe yourself gently and wrap yourself in the towel. Feel the warmth of the towel around you.

Cold bath gives your body a 'cold water shock', which can kickstart the immune system by producing white blood cells and antioxidants.

Feel refreshed and get ready to rock!

Time taken for this activity: 10 to 15 minutes

‘The replenishing thing that comes with a nap: you end up with two mornings in a day.’

Pete Hamill

Take a Nap

It's nap time.

Let the world wait!

It's time for you to take a pause. Leave all the work in hand. Find a place to lie comfortably or pull a chair to sit back and relax. Look out for an eye mask or a handkerchief to cover your eyes. Set the alarm for 10 minutes, as it's an ideal time for a nap.

Lie down or sit back on the chair, close your eyes, put on the eye mask and slowly bring your attention to your breath. Take a deep breath and feel the body's movement; inflate the abdomen with inhalation and deflate it when you exhale.

With each deep breath, relax more and more. Relax each part of your body from head to toe. Feel the wave of relaxation touching each part of your body, starting from your head, and moving down to your face, neck, shoulder, chest, arms, spine, stomach, pelvic area, thighs, knee, calf, feet and toe. Pay attention to each body part and keep relaxing them on your way down from head to toe. Relax each joint of the body.

Feel lighter and lighter; visualise yourself as light as a bubble floating in the air. Keep your eyes closed and focus on your breath till the alarm rings.

When the alarm rings, gently open your eyes and switch off the alarm. Wash your face with water, drink a glass of water, and return to work, recharged and refreshed.

A short nap can boost memory, improve job performance, lift your mood, make you more alert, and ease stress.

Time taken for this activity: 10 to 15 minutes

‘Close your eyes, clear your heart and let your spirit dance.

The music within you is sufficient.’

Dance Without Music

Time to dance. Get up and get ready to dance.

Think of a place where you can be with yourself for some time without any distractions. If you don't find such a place, happily move to the washroom and lock yourself in for some time.

You can do this activity either sitting or standing. If doing it in a sitting position, the focus will be more on the upper body; if doing it while standing, the whole body can be used. No music is needed, as you will create your music and rhythm during this activity.

Once you have found a comfortable place, relax. Close your eyes, take a deep breath, smile gently, and raise both hands above your head. Hold them in this position for 5 seconds and slowly bring them down while moving your hands in circular dance movements. Repeat it five times.

Think of a dance movement with your hands and let your feet join in. Remember to keep your eyes closed during this activity. Enjoy being in your present. Keep dancing.

Keep changing the moves and adding new ones. Use your creativity to beautify your dance.

Visualise a flower in the breeze, moving with the wind, dancing to the flow of current, going in every direction slowly and smoothly. Be that flower and flow with the wind. Enjoy the breeze and be in the moment.

When you are comfortable, stop and open your eyes. Take a deep breath, smile and move on to rock the world.

Time taken for this activity: 10 to 15 minutes

‘Believe in your #selfie.

When in doubt,
Pout it out.’

Take a Selfie

Time for a selfie. Get ready to face yourself.

Take out your mobile or switch on the webcam on your computer. Change it to selfie mode. Look into the camera and smile. Hold your smile for 5 seconds. Observe yourself closely on the screen. See the smiling lines on your face. Observe your eyes, eyebrows, cheeks and hair. Observe your appearance, dress, jewellery, makeup, and hairstyle.

Observe your background and different objects around you, and notice the colour of the things in the picture. Find a better place if you want, with better lighting and surroundings. Once you are OK, look straight into the camera, smile and click your picture. Open the photo and see yourself smiling. Imitate the image and make the same pose as in the photo.

Now make a pout, hold for some time, observe and when you feel OK, click your picture. Open your photo and make the same pose as in the image. Give a flying kiss to your photo.

Now, pose differently, eyebrows up and eyes wide open, mouth open with amazement, and hand on your cheek. Observe your posture for some time and when OK, click the picture. Open your photo, make the same surprising pose and smile.

Now, make a laughing pose, mouth wide open with a big smile, eyes small in size, cheeks tightened, teeth visible, and head tilted a bit. Observe your posture for a while and click the picture when you feel it is OK. Open your photo, make the same laughing pose and appreciate yourself.

Close your eyes and remember all these pics; when comfortable, open your eyes and get ready to rock the world.

Time taken for this activity: 5 to 10 minutes

‘If you want to see a rainbow, you have to learn to see the rain.’

Paulo Coelho

Watch a Video of Rainfall

Time to turn to the screen and get soaked in the beauty of rain.

Search for a soothing video of rainfall on your mobile, TV or computer. In the search window, search for relaxing rain videos without music. Find a video that appeals to your eyes and ears.

Play the video in full-screen mode. Turn on the volume to a comfortable level; if you have earphones, just put them on. Be at a comfortable distance from your screen and free your hands.

Take a deep breath and relax. Keep watching the rainfall video, and observe the rain, the wind, the rain drops and each movement in the video with the rain. Hear the sound of the wind, thunder and raindrops falling on the earth. Keep watching for 1 minute, and then close your eyes. Keep your focus on the sound of rain, wind and thunder and visualise the entire video with closed eyes. Keep smiling during the activity.

Think of some pleasant memories of rain and return to those memories. It can be a memory of an enjoyable trip in the rain, playing in the shower or a rain dance, etc. . Relive those lovely memories of rain.

Smell the aroma of fresh raindrops falling on the dry earth—the unique, fresh, calming, earthy scent in the rain shower. Smell the earthy aroma. Keep your eyes closed and visualise yourself going under the rain. Feel the raindrops touching your skin, rolling over each part of your body, starting from the head and slowly moving down. Drenching you with its flow—the soothing sound of raindrops touching the ground. Stay in the rain for some time.

When you feel comfortable, open your eyes. Wash your face with fresh water, feel refreshed and get back to work.

Time taken for this activity: 5 to 10 minutes

‘Journaling is like whispering to one’s self and listening at the same time.’

Mina Murray

Do Journaling

Time for journaling!

Get ready to spend some quality time with yourself. Grab a pen and Paper, and avoid using a pencil or any electronic device for this activity. Switch off your gadgets and keep them aside. Sit at a comfortable place where you can be yourself and there are no distractions.

Take a deep breath, close your eyes and focus on your body. Observe what is going on in your mind and become aware of your thoughts. Close your eyes, scroll through your thoughts and select a thought you want to explore further. Just be with that thought and explore it.

When you are comfortable, open your eyes and take your pen. Start writing what comes to your mind. Connecting to the self and writing out your heart is a meditative process.

Don't stop to read or check what you have written. Just keep writing without judging. Be creative and make some drawings too. Your journal is your private place to express whatever you feel; it doesn't need to follow any particular format. Let the words and ideas flow freely. Don't worry about spelling mistakes or what other people might think.

When you have nothing to write, stop and keep your pen down. Close your eyes, take a deep breath, smile and be in the moment. Feel the changes in your body.

When you feel comfortable, open your eyes. Keep the Paper with you in a safe place, or if you don't want to keep it with you, just tear it off into small pieces and throw it in the trash.

Feel refreshed and get back to work!

Time taken for this activity: 10 to 15 minutes

‘What keeps life fascinating is the constant creativity of the soul.’

Deepak Chopra

Draw and Colour

Time to explore your creativity!

Take a pencil, Paper and some colours. You can use any colours of your choice, wax crayon, pencil colours, oil pastels or sketch colours. Sit at a comfortable place, close your eyes, relax and take a deep breath. Think of something that you can draw. It can be anything you can quickly put on Paper, some scenery, flowers, designs, etc. Visualise your drawing on the Paper.

Gently open your eyes and turn to your Paper. With your pencil in hand, start drawing. Be in the present moment and put your heart and soul into the drawing. Draw what comes to your mind without a second thought; be in the flow. Avoid using an eraser, and feel free to make mistakes. Enjoying the process is more important than perfection.

Once the drawing is complete, start colouring it. Go ahead: colour outside the lines! It can be as neat — or as messy — as you choose. Use the colours of your choice and enjoy the process. Complete colouring the whole drawing or leave it incomplete as per your choice.

Once you are satisfied, relax your hands and observe your creation. Try to interpret what is on Paper in front of you. See what colours you have used and how they represent your current state. Keep observing the drawing until you feel comfortable; feel free to add something.

Once you feel comfortable, keep the drawing safe and return to work.

Colouring has the ability to relax the brain. It induces the same state as meditating by reducing the thoughts of a restless mind.

Time taken for this activity: 5 to 10 minutes

‘Get lost in the nature and you will find yourself.’

Watch Nature Videos

Time to soak in the beauty of nature!

Search for a soothing nature video on your mobile, TV or computer. Find a video that appeals to your eyes and ears. In the search window, search for relaxing nature videos. Look out for the sceneries that make you feel calm; it can be a forest, water body, mountains, beach, etc.

Play the video in full-screen mode. Turn on the volume to a comfortable level; if you have earphones, just put them on. Be at a comfortable distance from your screen and free your hands.

Take a deep breath and relax. Keep watching the nature in the video, and observe the scenic beauty, the sun, the trees, the water bodies, the birds, and all the beautiful God-made things. Hear the sound of the wind, birds, water, etc., in the video. Keep observing for 1 minute and then close your eyes. Hear the soothing natural sounds and visualise the entire video. Recreate the screen in your mind with your eyes closed.

Think of some pleasant memories of a vacation at a beautiful place like this. Smile and go back to those sweet memories. Relive those lovely memories.

Keep your eyes close and visualise yourself going to the same place. Smell the fresh air aroma and wind blow in your hair. Stay in that place for some time.

When you feel comfortable, open your eyes. Wash your face with fresh water, feel refreshed and get back to work.

The positive effects of nature have been extensively studied, showing that interactions with natural settings reduce stress. Natural sounds help to restore mental fatigue

Time taken for this activity: 5 to 10 minutes

'Give God your weakness, and he'll give you his strength.'

Pray to God

Thank God! It's time to connect to the Almighty!

Just leave all work in hand, sit back, be comfortable and relax. Close your eyes, take a deep breath and join your hands in the prayer position.

Once you have selected the centre of your focus (God), start imagining it. Visualise your deity with your mind's eyes. If you do not have a figure in mind, then visualise a place where you feel at peace. It can be any place outside your home or inside your home, where you often visit to feel at ease. If you can't think of anything, then visualise the sun, moon, stars or sky.

Pay attention and be in your present. Go into each tiny detail of what you are visualising. Observe the shape, size, colour, texture, and appearance. Smell the fragrance. Experience the emotions that are popping up, and acknowledge and accept them.

Take a deep breath and calm yourself more and more with each breath.

Start with a thank you note, and thank God for whatever good you have in your life. Thank God for whatever you have received from them, and keep a gentle smile while thanking him. Thank God for blessing you with human life, with the power to smile. If you have any requests, present your requests to God with hope and trust in your heart.

Once you feel satisfied, pray to show you the right path in the future, giving you the power to deal with challenges, solve problems, and empower you to live happily.

Time taken for this activity: 3 to 5 minutes

‘Clap for yourself, even if no one is clapping for you!’

Clap for 30 Seconds

Get ready for a big round of applause!

Get up and find a place to comfortably clap without disturbing others. It can be a room where you can lock the door or an open space like a park. If you can't find any such place, lock yourself in the washroom. After all, washrooms are our best friends.

Once you are at a place where you can be comfortable, you can either sit or stand at your convenience. Close your eyes, smile gently, slowly take a deep breath and relax.

Bring both your hands in front of you and join them. Touch the tips of the fingers of both hands and the palm. Now move your hands away and join them again with a clap. The hand posture should remain intact (tips to tips and palm to palm).

If you are wearing any rings, try to remove them and place them safely somewhere. Keep your eyes closed if possible, and keep increasing the clapping speed. Clap non-stop for 30 seconds.

After 30 seconds, stop and keep your hands joined. Close your eyes, smile and feel the sensation in your hands. Feel the warmth between your hands. Gently rub your hands until you feel the heat, and put your hands on your eyes. Hold it there for five seconds. Rub your palms again and put them on the crown of your head, holding it there for five seconds. Feel the energy flowing down from your hands to your body.

Experience positive changes in the body. Smile and open your eyes gently.

Time taken for this activity: 1 to 2 minutes

‘Add positivity to your life, and positive things will happen.’

Write Plus Sign (+)

Time to think positively!

Take a pen and Paper. Find an appropriate place, free of distractions, where you can sit comfortably and write.

Sit back and relax. Close your eyes, take a slow deep breath, and calm yourself more and more with each breath. Be in this state for some time. Once you are comfortable, open your eyes, take your pen and start making Plus sign on the Paper.

+ + + + + + + + + + + + + + +

You can make it anywhere on the Paper. Make it anywhere on paper, randomly or in a sequence per your wish. Make it of any size, small or big.

While making a plus sign on the Paper: say these words 'Be positive'.

Speak it with a slightly loud volume so that you can hear your voice. Focus on what you write, what you speak and what you hear. Pay attention to each tiny detail and observe.

Keep writing it till you are short of space. If you want, you can take another sheet to continue writing.

Once you feel satisfied, stop writing and hold the paper in front of you.

Feel the positive energy from the Paper as you observe it. Look at each plus sign and say, "Be Positive".

Observe your feelings now, and feel more confident, motivated and stress-free.

Time taken for this activity: 3 to 5 minutes

‘Imagine smiling after a slap in the face. Then think of doing it twenty-four hours a day.’

Markus Zusak

Slap Yourself

Time to stop overthinking!

Get up and move to the washroom. Lock yourself. Connect to yourself and bring to your awareness the most disturbing thoughts that continuously occupy your mind-thoughts you want to eliminate.

Look into the mirror, look into your eyes and feel the emotions associated with the thoughts. Think of any possible good outcome of these thoughts.

Ask yourself these questions:

- Are these thoughts helping you in any way?
- Is there a better alternative thought that can replace these disturbing thoughts?
- Do you want to stop these thoughts from disturbing you?

Once you are ready with the answers. It's time to work on programming your mind to control these thoughts.

Sit down and become aware of your thoughts again; the moment the disturbing thoughts come to your mind, slap yourself and say 'STOP It'. Depending on the intensity of the emotion, you can hit hard or slow.

Slap once and stop; the moment the disturbing thought again comes to your mind, slap yourself and say, 'stop it.'

Continue the process until the thought stops coming, or do it a minimum of 7 times.

Don't stop your tears if they come out. Cry if you feel like it.

Once done, close your eyes, feel the sensations in your body, and notice the positive changes. When you are comfortable, open your eyes and get back to work.

Don't slap yourself for self-harm; use this technique only as a stress buster.

Time taken for this activity: 3 to 5 minutes

'The energy of the mind is the essence of life.'

Aristotle

Energize Crown Chakra

Time to energise!

Leave all work in hand. Sit back and relax. Close your eyes and take a deep breath. Focus on breathing, and observe the body movement with each breath; with inhalation, the stomach should inflate, and with exhalation, it should deflate. Sync your body movement with the breath. Count your breaths in your mind and take ten deep breaths.

Keeping your eyes closed, rub your palms together till a count of 15. Now, put both palms on the top of your head where we put the crown. This place is known as the crown chakra. Touch your crown chakra with both hands and hold. Observe the sensation in the head and feel the energy flowing down from the top, moving down to your face and spreading towards your chest area.

Hold it there until you feel comfortable, keep your eyes closed, smile gently and take slow, deep breaths.

Be in this position for at least 1 minute. Slowly open your eyes and bring your hands down when you feel comfortable. Once more, rub your palms for 15 seconds and put them on your crown chakra, this time, you can keep your eyes open. Take slow and deep breaths and have a smile on your face.

Be in this pose for at least 30 seconds. When you feel comfortable, slowly bring your hands down. Close your eyes and place both hands on your thighs with palms open and facing up. Feel the changes in your body. Notice the feeling of positivity.

Gently open your eyes, feel refreshed and get up!

Time taken for this activity: 2 to 3 minutes

'Life is a roller coaster. You can either scream every time you hit a bump or you can throw your hands up in the air and enjoy it.'

Hands Up & Move Around

Time to open up to the universe!

Leave all your work, close your eyes and remain still in the position in which you currently are. Hold and stay there without any movement. Keep your eyes closed, raise both your hands, keep them stretched above your head and move your face towards the sky; stay comfortably in this position until you feel OK.

Slowly bring your hands down and come back to your usual pose. Gently open your eyes and keep a smile on your face.

Now, look for a place where you can comfortably stand and move in rounds. Find a safe area to move around 360 degrees with closed eyes. Once ready, go to the desired place and place yourself safely.

You have to stand for this activity. When you are comfortably placed, close your eyes, take a slow and deep breath, slowly raise your hands, keep them comfortably stretched above your head and hold it there. Be in this position for 10 seconds and slowly start turning around and taking small rounds.

You can also move your head backwards to be more comfortable. Move slowly and gently. Take as many rounds as you feel comfortable, but not less than five rounds.

When you feel OK, stop, bring your hands down, smile gently, keep your eyes closed and feel the changes in your body. Feel light and at peace.

Time taken for this activity: 2 to 3 minutes

‘Life is a collage of events.’

Mohanlal

Make Paper Collage

Time to collate!

Stop everything and think of paper collages you have seen in your life. If you can't think of one, take the help of google. Spend 1 minute on google to get an idea of how to make a paper collage. Remember, it's just for fun; no need to be perfect.

Grab various papers, including paper scraps, magazines or newspaper cuttings, colourful sheets, etc. Take some A4 sheets, which will be used as the base for making the collage. It can be white or different coloured. Take glue and scissors.

Once you are ready with the material, sit down and take a deep breath. Relax and bring your attention to the paper collage activity. Visualise how you want to make it and the final look.

Start with a base sheet on which you will paste the collage. Cut or tear the strips of Paper in different shapes and sizes. You can cut it with scissors or tear it from both sides; you can also cut it from one side and tear it from the other. Cut different coloured paper strips as you like. You can also cut additional photos or letters from the magazine to make the collage.

Now, start pasting the cut-outs on the base sheet. Make layers, and paste until you like the look. You can paste colourful strips first, and then on top of it, paste the images. You can also paste letters to make a specific word you want.

Keep pasting the paper pieces until you are satisfied with the final look.

You can also draw something over the collage to give it a better look. Keep adding paper cuttings on each corner of the Paper. Make it as colourful and beautiful as you can with your efforts.

Once done, stop and take a look at your art piece. Bring a gentle smile on your face, and appreciate it and yourself. Close your eyes and feel the changes in your body. Keep smiling, and get ready to rock!

Time taken for this activity: 5 to 10 minutes

‘You are the writer of your own story’.

Create a Personal Life Story

Time to work on yourself!

Get ready to be the hero of the story you will write. Yes, your own life story.

Leave all work in hand and find a place where you can be yourself. Take a pen and Paper along with you. Sit back, relax, close your eyes and take five deep breaths. Open your eyes and bring your attention to the activity. Remember, this activity is only for fun, so think about whatever comes to mind. Think about your dream life and how you desire your life to be going ahead. A dream can be anything, possible or not possible.

Once you have visualised your life story for your future, take your pen and start writing on the Paper. Think of all the positive things that you want for yourself and write them down. Write what you want in your life, what you want to be, and how you see yourself in the future.

When you feel comfortable, close your eyes and visualise further. Keep adding to the story. You can add imaginary objects, places, people, events and all that comes to your mind.

Take your time and be slow in thinking, visualising and writing it down. Try to write as many details as you can. When you feel fulfilled, stop writing. Bring a gentle smile, close your eyes and take slow deep breaths.

When you feel comfortable, open your eyes and read what you have written. Try not to edit while reading; just read and appreciate the personal life story that you have created for yourself. Keep a smile on your face while reading.

When done, close the papers, keep them aside, close your eyes, take a deep breath and observe the changes in your body. Feel the sensations and positive changes.

Open your eyes when you feel comfortable, and get ready to rock!

Time taken for this activity: 10 to 15 minutes

‘Happiness isn’t about getting what you want always.

It's about loving what you have and being grateful for it.’

Make Gratitude Journal

Time to be grateful!

Leave all work in hand, sit back and relax.

Find a pen and Paper (try to find a new notebook that can be used again for the same activity in future). Look for a place where you can be yourself and there is a minimum distraction.

Once you settle down, close your eyes, take slow deep breaths, connect to your body, and bring your attention to your present. Engage your mind to think of the things you are grateful for. Keep thinking and reflecting for 30 seconds, and then start writing.

Start by writing, " I am thankful to.....". Next, ponder why you feel gratitude for them and complete the sentence "I am thankful to... for... ".

For example, "I am thankful to my mother for giving me life and love."

Reflect on the reason for being grateful and write as much as possible. Keep adding to this list, and write at least five things you would like to thank for being a part of your life. Be generous in thanking. Make a list of at least five gratitude statements. Be grateful for any person, event, or idea, big or small. Continue writing as long and as much as you want.

Once done, close your eyes, smile gently, take a slow breath, put one hand on your heart, think of the list you have made and slowly say thank you to them.

Gently open your eyes and feel the changes in your body.

Time taken for this activity: 5 to 10 minutes

‘Talk to yourself once in a day, otherwise you may miss meeting an excellent person in this world.’

Swami Vivekanand

Talk to Yourself

Time to meet yourself!

Look for a place where you can be yourself with minimum distractions.

Once you settle down, close your eyes, take slow deep breaths, connect to your body, and bring your attention to your present. Start observing your thoughts, analyse what is going on in your mind, and spend 30 seconds just sitting and watching. Imagine yourself sitting in front of you- blindly trust this person and feel free to open up.

Start sharing everything that comes to your mind. Keep your volume low while speaking. Pause to think and vent out completely. Don't overthink before sharing; after all, you are only listening. Call yourself by your name and use 'you' instead of 'I' while addressing yourself.

Remember, you have to play the role of both persons in this exercise. Not only the part of the speaker who speaks out their heart but also the listener who is engaged in listening and may have to speak when the need arises.

You can ask questions to yourself and seek answers. For example, ask yourself, 'Will I succeed?' or 'Is there any other way out?' etc. While answering, you may come across a call for action. If such things happen, then make a note of it.

You can also give yourself instructions when the need arises. Give clear instructions as to what should be done instead of saying you will do well.

Do not dwell too much on negativity. Talk positively and use optimistic language.

Once you feel satisfied, stop talking, close your eyes, take deep breaths, put one hand on your heart and say thank you to yourself.

Gently open your eyes and feel the changes in your body.

Time taken for this activity: 5 to 10 minutes

Personal Resources to De-stress

'People have the inner resources to become anything they want to be. Challenge just becomes the vehicle for tapping into those inner resources.' Erik Weihenmayer

Use these pages to make notes of the resources, methods and ways that have helped you to break free during difficult times.

Be as creative as you can, to note down in your own way.